Conversational
Yiddish
Quick and Easy

YATIR NITZANY

Dedication

To all those who ever struggled with learning a
foreign language and to Wolfgang Karfunkel

Also by Yatir Nitzany

Conversational Spanish Quick and Easy

....

Conversational French Quick and Easy

....

Conversational Italian Quick and Easy

....

Conversational Portuguese Quick and Easy

....

Conversational German Quick and Easy

....

Conversational Russian Quick and Easy

....

Conversational Hebrew Quick and Easy

....

Conversational Polish Quick and Easy

....

Conversational Arabic Quick and Easy
Palestinian Dialect

....

Conversational Arabic Quick and Easy
Lebanese Dialect

....

Conversational Arabic Quick and Easy
Egyptian Dialect

Foreword

About Myself

For many years I struggled to learn Spanish, and I still knew no more than about twenty words. Consequently, I was extremely frustrated. One day I stumbled upon this method as I was playing around with word combinations. Suddenly, I came to the realization that every language has a certain core group of words that are most commonly used and, simply by learning them, one could gain the ability to engage in quick and easy conversational Spanish.

I discovered which words those were, and I narrowed them down to three hundred and fifty that, once memorized, one could connect and create one's own sentences. The variations were and are *infinite*! By using this incredibly simple technique, I could converse at a proficient level and speak Spanish. Within a week, I astonished my Spanish-speaking friends with my newfound ability. The next semester I registered at my university for a Spanish language course, and I applied the same principles I had learned in that class (grammar, additional vocabulary, future and past tense, etc.) to those three hundred and fifty words I already had memorized, and immediately I felt as if I had grown wings and learned how to fly.

At the end of the semester, we took a class trip to San José, Costa Rica. I was like a fish in water, while the rest of my classmates were floundering and still struggling to converse. Throughout the following months, I again applied the same principle to other languages—French, Portuguese, Italian, and Arabic, all of which I now speak proficiently, thanks to this very simple technique.

This method is by far the fastest way to master quick and easy conversational language skills. There is no other technique that compares to my concept. It is effective, it worked for me, and it will work for you. Be consistent with my program, and you too will succeed the way I and many, many others have.

Contents

INTRODUCTION TO
THE PROGRAM

People often dream about learning a foreign language, but usually they never do it. Some feel that they just won't be able to do it while others believe that they don't have the time. Whatever your reason is, it's time to set that aside. With my new method, you will have enough time, and you will not fail. You will actually learn how to speak the fundamentals of the language—fluently in as little as a few days. Of course, you won't speak perfect Yiddish at first, but you will certainly gain significant proficiency. For example, if you travel to Brooklyn or Israel, you will almost effortlessly be able engage in basic conversational communication with the locals in the present tense and you will no longer be intimidated by culture shock. It's time to relax. Learning a language is a valuable skill that connects people of multiple cultures around the world—and you now have the tools to join them.

How does my method work? I have taken twenty-seven of the most commonly used languages in the world and distilled from them the three hundred and fifty most frequently used words in any language. This process took three years of observation and research, and during that time, I determined which words I felt were most important for this method of basic conversational communication. In that time, I chose these words in such a way that they were structurally interrelated and that, when combined, form sentences. Thus, once you succeed in memorizing these words, you will be able to combine these words and form your own sentences. The words are spread over twenty pages. The words will also combine easily in sentences, for example, enabling you to ask simple questions, make basic statements, and obtain a rudimentary understanding of others' communications. In fact, there are just nine basic words that will effectively build bridges, enabling you to speak in an understandable manner (please see Building Bridges). I have also created Memorization Made Easy techniques for this program in order to help with the memorization of the vocabulary. Please also see Pronunciation of the ch in order to gain proficiency in the reading and pronunciation of the Yiddish language prior to starting this program.

My book is mainly intended for basic present tense vocal communication, meaning anyone can easily use it to "get by" linguistically while visiting a foreign country without learning the entire language. With practice, you will be 100 percent understandable to native speakers, which is your aim. One disclaimer: this is not a grammar book, though it does address minute and essential grammar rules. Therefore, understanding complex sentences with obscure words in Yiddish is beyond the scope of this book.

People who have tried this method have been successful, and by the time you finish this book, you will understand and be understood in basic conversational Yiddish. This is the best basis to learn not only the Yiddish language but any language. This is an entirely revolutionary, no-fail concept, and your ability to combine the pieces of the "language puzzle" together will come with great ease.

This is the best program that was ever designed to teach the reader how to become conversational. Other conversational programs will only teach you phrases. But this is the only program that will teach you how to create your own sentences for the purpose of becoming conversational.

The Yiddish Language

Written with Hebrew alphabet characters, Yiddish is a High German language that was used by Jews from central and eastern Europe before the Holocaust. Most likely beginning around the ninth century CE, Yiddish was developed over the course of several centuries by Ashkenazi Jews in the Holy Roman Empire. Yiddish combined a Germanic language base with some Aramaic, Hebrew, Slavic, and even a smattering of Romance language words to create a distinct patois that served to unite diverse Jewish populations in Europe following the Diaspora. As Jewish communities grew in Europe, the Yiddish language grew with them, eventually including as many as ten to thirteen million speakers. However, the deaths of six million Jews in the Holocaust and the subsequent dispersal of Jewish communities following World War II decimated the ranks of Yiddish speakers in the twentieth century, and currently, it is estimated that as few as two million people worldwide still speak Yiddish. Nonetheless, some Yiddish words have been absorbed by many of the languages with which Yiddish cultures interacted following World War II (including chutzpah, glitch, kitsch, klutz, kosher, schtum, schmooze, and verklempt, among others, in English). Today, the language is enjoying a resurgence in Hasidic Jewish communities where it is the primary language spoken.

MEMORIZATION MADE EASY

There is no doubt the three hundred and fifty words in my program are the required essentials in order to engage in quick and easy basic conversation in any foreign language. However, some people may experience difficulty in the memorization. For this reason, I created Memorization Made Easy. This memorization technique will make this program so simple and fun that it's unbelievable! I have spread the words over the following twenty pages. Each page contains a vocabulary table of ten to fifteen words. Below every vocabulary box, sentences are composed from the words on the page that you have just studied. This aids greatly in memorization. Once you succeed in memorizing the first page, then proceed to the second page. Upon completion of the second page, go back to the first and review. Then proceed to the third page. After memorizing the third, go back to the first and second and repeat. And so on. As you continue, begin to combine words and create your own sentences in your head. Every time you proceed to the following page, you will notice words from the previous pages will be present in those simple sentences as well, because repetition is one of the most crucial aspects in learning any foreign language. Upon completion of your twenty pages, *congratulations*, you have absorbed the required words and gained a basic, quick-and-easy proficiency and you should now be able to create your own sentences and say anything you wish in the Yiddish language. This is a crash course in conversational Yiddish, and it works!

THE YIDDISH *CH* PRONUNCIATION

Ch - For certain languages including Yiddish, Hebrew, Arabic, Farsi, Pashto, Urdu, Hindi, etc., and also German, to properly pronounce the *ch* or *kh* is essential, for example, *Khaled* (a Muslim name) or *Chanukah* (a Jewish holiday) or *Nacht* ("night" in German). The best way to describe *ch* or *kh* is to say "ka" or "ha" while at the same time putting your tongue at the back of your throat and blowing air. It's pronounced similarly to the sound that you make when clearing your throat. Please remember this whenever you come across any word containing a *ch* in this program.

NOTE TO THE READER

The purpose of this book is merely to enable you to communicate in the Yiddish language. In the program itself (pages 17-39) you may notice that the composition of some of those sentences might sound rather clumsy. This is intentional. These sentences were formulated in a specific way to serve two purposes: to facilitate the easy memorization of the vocabulary and to teach you how to combine the words in order to form your own sentences for quick and easy communication, rather than making complete literal sense in the English language. So keep in mind that this is not a phrase book!

As the title suggests, the sole purpose of this program is for conversational use only. It is based on the mirror translation technique. These sentences, as well as the translations are not incorrect, just a little clumsy. Latin languages, Semitic languages, and Anglo-Germanic languages, as well as a few others, are compatible with the mirror translation technique.

Many users say that this method surpasses any other known language learning technique that is currently out there on the market. Just stick with the program and you will achieve wonders!

Again, I wish to stress this program is by no means, shape, or form a phrase book! The sole purpose of this book is to give you a fundamental platform to enable you to connect certain words to become conversational. Please also read the "Introduction" and the "About Me" section prior to commencing the program.

In order to succeed with my method, please start on the very first page of the program and fully master one page at a time prior to proceeding to the next. Otherwise, you will overwhelm yourself and fail. Please do not skip pages, nor start from the middle of the book.

It is a myth that certain people are born with the talent to learn a language, and this book disproves that myth. With this method, anyone can learn a foreign language as long as he or she follows these explicit directions:

* Memorize the vocabulary on each page

* Follow that memorization by using a notecard to cover the words you have just memorized and test yourself.

* Then read the sentences following that are created from the vocabulary bank that you just mastered.

* Once fully memorized, give yourself the green light to proceed to the next page.

Again, if you proceed to the following page without mastering the previous, you are guaranteed to gain nothing from this book. If you follow the prescribed steps, you will realize just how effective and simplistic this method is.

THE PROGRAM

Let's Begin! "Vocabulary"
(memorize the vocabulary)

I | I am	E'ech | e'ech bin
With you	Mit deer
With him / with her	Mit aim / mit eer
With us	Mit intz
For you	Far deir, *(formal)* far ir
Without him	Oo'n aim
Without them	Nisht meit'zai
Always	Shten'dik
Was	Gev'ain, iz gev'ain
This, This is	Duce, dem
Is / it's / is it?	Iz / es iz / iz es
Sometimes	Am'oole
Maybe	Heint, efsher
You are/ are you?	Bist du (or) di bist?
Better	Besser
You	Du, di / *(formal)* ir/ *(plural)* alle
Today	Haynt
From	Fin *(or)* foon

Sentences from the vocabulary (now you can speak the sentences and connect the words)

This is for you
Duce iz far deir

I am from Germany
E'ech bin fin Deushland

Are you from Israel?
Du bist fin Isruel?

I am with you
E'ech bin mit deir

Sometimes you are with us at the house
Amaol bist ir mit ins in shteeb

I am always with her
E'ech bin shten'dik mit eer

Are you without them today?
Bist ir Nisht mit'zai haynt?

Sometimes I am with him
Am'oole e'ech bin Mit aim

*Nisht mit literally means "not with."

I was	E'ech bein gev'ain
To be	Tse'zain
The	Di
Same / like *(as in similar)*	Zelbe
Good	Git
Here	Do
Very	Zeyer
And	Aun
Between	Tsvishn
Now	Yetst
Later / After / afterwards	Shpeter / noch
If	Oi'bb
Yes	Yo
Day	Toog
Tomorrow	Morgen
Then	Demolt
Also / too / as well	Aoych, ochet

Between now and later
tsvishn yetst aun shpeter
If it's later, then it is better tomorrow
Oi'bb iz shpeter, demolt es iz beser morgn
This is also good
duce iz aoych git
This is the same
Duce iz di zelbe
Yes, you are very good
yo, di bist zeyer git
I was here with them
E'ech bein gev'ain do mit zei
The same day
Di zelbe toog

Afterwards	Shpeter
Ok	Okay
Even if	Afil'e
No	La
Worse	Erger'e
Where	Vu, vi, ve'er
Everything	Alles / alts
Somewhere	Ergets
What	Vus?
Almost	Shi'a
There	Dort
I go	E'ech geyn

Afterwards is worse
Shpeter iz erger'e
Even if I go now
Afil'e oi'bb e'ech geyn yetst
Where is everything?
Vi iz alles?
Maybe somewhere
Efsher ergets
What? I am almost there
Vus? Eech bin shi'a dort
Where are you?
Vu bist du?
You and I
Di aun e'ech

House	Hoyz, shteeb/ haym (home)
In, at, at the,in the	In (or) ba
Car	Vugen/ auto/ mashin
Already	Shoiin
Good morning	Git Morgen
How are you?	Vas machstu?
Where are you from?	Fin vi bista
But/however	Ober (or) iber
Hello	Hi
What is your name?	Vus iz deyn numen?
How old are you?	Vi alt zenen di?
Son	Zun
Daughter	Tochter
Your	Deyn
Doesn't / isn't	Nisht
Hard / easy	Shver / lae'echt
Still	Doch
He / She	Er / zi

She is without a car, so maybe she is still at the house?

Zi iz oo'n vugen, azoy afshr **zi** iz doch in di hoyz?

I am already in the car with your son and your daughter

E'ech bein shoiin in di auto mit deyn zun aun deyn tochter

Good morning, how are you today?

Git morgn, vas machstu haynt ?

Hello, what is your name?

Hi, vos iz deyn nomen?

This is very hard, but it's not easy

Das iz zeyer shver, ober iz nisht lae'echt

Thank you	Danke shein/ dinke shein
For	Far
Anything	Alles
That, That is	Duce iz
Thanks	Dank
A	Ein / a
No/ Not	Nein / nisht
I am not	E'ech bin nisht
Away	Avek
Late	Shpater
Similar, like	Endlech
Another/ Other	Ander'e
Side	Zayt
Until	Biz
Yesterday	Nachten
Without us	Nisht mit intz
Since	Vayl, zint
Day	Toog
Before	Fryer

Thanks for anything
Dank far alles
It's almost time
Ez iz shi'a di tsa'yt
I am not here, I am away
E'ech bein nisht du, e'ech bin avek
That is a similar house
Duce hoyz iz endlech
I am from the other side
E'ech bein fin di ander'e zayt
But I was here until late yesterday
Ober eech bein gevain du biz shpater nachten
Since the other day
Vayl di ander'e toog

I say / I am saying	E'ech zoog
What time is it?	Vos iz du tsa'yt
I want	E'ech vil
Without you	Oo'n dir
Everywhere /wherever	Überall
I am going	E'ech gey
With	Mit
My	Mein
Cousin	Kuzin/(P)Kusinkes
I Must	E'ech mizz
I need	E'ech darf
Time	Tsa'yt
Night	Nacht
To see	Zen
Light	Le'echt
Outside	Draussen / aroys
Without	Oo'n
Happy	Gleeklech
I see / I am seeing	E'ech zei

I am saying no / I say no
E'ech zoog nisht
I want to see this in the daytime
E'ech vil zen duce ba toog
I see this everywhere
E'ech zei duce uberall
I am happy without my cousins here
E'ech bin gleeklech oo'n meyn kuzinkes do
I need to be there at night
E'ech daff tuzayn dort ba nacht
I see light outside
E'ech zei le'echt draussen
What time is it right now?
Vos iz du tsa'yt yetst?

*This *isn't* a phrase book! The purpose of this book is *solely* to provide you with the tools to create *your own* sentences!

Place	Platz
Easy	Lae'echt
To find	Tsu gefinen
To look for/to search	Tsu ze'echen
Near / Close	Leiben / Nuent
To wait	Tsu varten
To sell	Tsu fakofein
To use	Tsu nitsen
To know	Tsu visn
To decide	Tsu bashlusn
Both	Beyde
That (conjunction)	Az
To	Tsu

This place is easy to find
Duce platz iz lae'ech tsu gefinen
I need to look for you next to your car
E'ech darf tsu ze'echen leiben deyen auto
I am saying to wait until tomorrow
E'ech bin gezagat tsu varten biz morgen
It's easy to sell this table
Es iz lae'echt tsu farkoyfn duce tish
I want to use this
E'ech vil tsu nitsen duce
I must know where is the house
E'ech mizz visn vu iz di hoytz
I must decide between both places
E'ech mizz bashlusn tsvishn beyde platz
I need to know that everything is OK
E'ech darf tsu visn az alts iz g'it

Because	Vayl
To buy	Tsu koyfen
I can / Can I?	E'ech ken / ken e'ech?
Them, they, their	Zey / zey / zeyer
I like	E'ech glach
Book	Be'yech
Mine	Mayn
To understand	Tsu farshteyn
Problem / Problems	Problem
I do, I am doing	E'ech mach (or) E'ech tin
Of	foon
To look	Tsu kiken
Myself	Yech
Enough	Ginik / genug
Food / water	Essen / vasser
Each/ every	Yay'den / yeder
To have	Tsu hoben
To work	Tsu arbeten

I like this hotel because I want to look at the beach

E'ech glach duce hatel vayl e'ech vil tsu kiken oifen yam

I want to buy a bottle of water

E'ech vil koyfen a flashe foon vaser

I do it like this each day

E'ech mach duce yay'den toog

Both of them have enough food

Beyde foon zey hoben genug essen

That is the book and that book is mine

Duce iz di be'yech aun duce be'yech iz mayn

I need to understand the problem

E'ech darf tsu farshteyn di problem

From the hotel I have a view of the city

Fin di hotel e'ech hobn a meynung foon di shtut

I can work today

E'ech ken arbeten haynt

I do my homework

E'ech mach meyn lektsyes

*In Yiddish "at the" can be *oifen*.

24

I like	E'ech glach
There is / There are	Es iz / es zenen
Family	Mishpuch'e
Why	Vuss / far vuss
To say	Tsu zogn
Something	Epes
To go	Tsu geyn
Ready	Greyt
Soon	Balt
To work	Zu arbeiten
Who	Ver
Busy	Farnumen
Parents	Eltern
I Must	E'ech mizz
Important	Ve'echtik

I like to be at home with my parents
E'ech glach tsu zeyn in shtyb mit meyn eltern
I want to know why I have to say something important
E'ech vil tsu visn vuss e'ech hobn tsu zogn epes ve'echtik
I am there with him
E'ech bin dort mit aim
I am busy, but I need to be ready soon
E'ech bin farnumen, ober e'ech darf tsu zeyn greyt balt
I like to work
E'ech glach tsu arbeiten
Who is there?
Ver iz dort?
I want to know if they are here, because I want to go outside
E'ech vil tsu visn aoyb zey zenen do, vayl e'ech vil tsu geyn
drossen/aroys
There are seven dolls
Es zenen zibn daltz

How much /How many	Vi fil
To take	Tsu nemen
With me	Mit mir
Instead	Enshtot
Only	Nor
When	Ven
Money	Gelt
Or	Oder
Were	Zenen
Without me	Oo'n me'in
Fast	Shnel
Slow	Pamelach / langsam'
Cold	Kalt
Inside	In
To eat	Tsu essen
Hot	Ha'ys
To Drive	Tsu furen

How much money do I need to take?

Vi fil gelt e'ech darf tsu nemen?

Instead of this cake, I like that cake

Enshtot dem leikach, e'ech glach duce leikach

Only when you can

Nor ven ir ken

They were without me yesterday

Zey zenen nisht mit mir nechtn

I need to drive the car very fast or very slowly

E'ech darf tsu furen di mashin zeyer shnel oder zeyer pamelach

It is very cold in the library

Si zeya kalt in di biblyotek

Yes, I like to eat this hot for my lunch

Yo, e'ech vil essen duce ha'ys far meyn mitoog

Nisht mit literally means "not with."

26

To answer	Tsu entfern
To fly	Tsu fleegen
Time	Mol
To travel	Tsu arumforn
To learn	Tsu lernen
How	Vi
To swim	Tsu shvimen
To practice	Tsu fir
To play	Tsu shpiln
To leave (something)	Tsu lozn
Many /much /a lot	Fil / fil / a plats
I go to	E'ech geyn tsu
First	Ershter
World	Velt
Children	Kinder

I need to answer many questions
E'ech darf tsu entfern fil shalus
I want to fly today
E'ech vil tsu fleegen haynt
I need to learn to swim
E'ech darf tsu lernen tsu shvimen
I want to know everything about how to play better tennis
E'ech vil tsu visn alts vegn vi tsu shpiln beser tenis
I want to leave this here for you, when I go to travel the world
E'ech vil tsu lozn dem do far ir, ven e'ech geyn tsu arumforn di velt
Since the first time
Zint di ershter mol
The children are yours
Di kinder zenen deyn

*With the knowledge you've gained so far, now try to create your own sentences!

Nobody / Anyone	Keinamen / keyner
Against	Kegen
Us	Aintz
To visit	Tsu furen
Mom / Mother	Momy
To give	Tsu gebn
Which	Vos
To meet	Tsu trefn
Someone	Emetser
Just	Nor
To walk	Tsu ga'yn
Week	Voch
Towards	Tovards
Than	Vi
Nothing	Gornisht
Around	Arim
On	Aoyf

Something is better than nothing
Epes iz beser vi gornisht
I am against him
E'ech bin kegen aim
We go each week to visit my family
Mir geyn yeder voch tsu furen meyn mishpuch'e
I need to give you something
E'ech darf tsu gebn ir epes
Do you want to meet someone?
Ir vil tsu trefn emetser?
I am here also on Wednesdays
Aoych e'ech bin do aoyf vednesdays
You do this everyday?
Di mach duce yeden toog?
You need to walk around the house
Ir darf tsu ga'yn arim di shtyb

*Ir is the formal "you." However, ir can also be used to demonstrate the indirect object pronoun of the pronoun "you," the person who is actually affected by the action that is being carried out.
- "I need to give you something" / E'ech darf tsu gebn ir epes

I have	E'ech hab
Don't	Nisht
Friend	Fraynd
To borrow	Tsu borgn
To look like / resemble	Tsu kuken dezelba
Grandfather	Zeyde
To want	Tsu vil/ tsu visn
To stay	Tsu blaybn
To continue	Tsu forzetsn
Way (road, path)	Veig/ strasse / avek
Do you want ?	Di vist?
Like (preposition)	Vi
To show	Tsu vayzn
To prepare	Tsu tsugreytn
I am not going	E'ech bin nisht gegangen

Do you want to look like Arnold
Di vist tsu kuken dezelba vi Arnold
I want to borrow this book for my grandfather
E'ech vil tsu borgn duce be'yech far meyn zeyde
I want to drive and to continue on this way to my house
E'ech vil tsu foren aun tsu forzetsn aoyf dem veig tsu meyn hoyz
I have a friend, that's why I want to stay in Munich
E'ech hob a fraynt, far deim e'ech vil blaybn in minchen
I don't want to see anyone here
E'ech vilish zen keinamen do
I need to show you how to prepare breakfast
E'ech darf tsu vayzn ir vi tsu greytn frishtik
Why don't you have this book?
Far vuss oistanish duce be'yech?
That is incorrect, I don't need the car today
Duce es nisht richdik, e'ech darfish di mashin haynt

*In Yiddish to negate a verb, simply add the suffix *ish, nit,* or *nisht.*
- "I want" / *e'ech vil*
- "I don't want" / *e'ech vilish*
- "I need" / *e'ech darf*
- "I don't need" / *e'ech darfish*
*"That's why" is *far deim*
*"To have" is *hob.* "Don't have" is *ostanish.*

To remember	Tsu gedenken
Yiddish	Yiddish
Number	Numer
Hour	Sheh
Dark / darkness	Finster
About / on the	Vegn, aoyf
Grandmother	Boba
Five	Fin'if
Minute / Minutes	Meynut / minut
More	Meya
To think	Tsu trachtn / tracht
To do	Tsu tin / tsu ton
To come	Tsu kimen
To hear	Tsu her'n
Last	Let'ste
To talk / To Speak	Tsu reden/ shprechen

I need to remember your number

E'ech darf tsu gedenken deyn numer

This is the last hour of darkness

Das iz di let'ste sheh foon fintsternish

I want to come and to hear my grandmother speak Yiddish today

E'ech vil tsu kimen aun tsu her'n meyn boba reden yiddish haynt

I need to think more about this, and what to do

E'ech darf tsu trachtn mer vegn dem, aun vos tsu tin

From here to there, it's only five minutes

Fin do tsu dorten, es iz nor fin'if minut

Early	Fri'et
Germany	Deutshland
Tonight	Haynt ba nacht
German	Deusch
To bring	Tsu brengen
To try	Tsu prubirn
To rent	Tsu dingen
Without her	Oo'n eer
We are	Mir zenen
To turn off	Faloshen
To ask	Tsu fregn
To stop	Tsu halten
Permission	Derloybenish
Beach	Yam

He needs to leave and rent a house on the beach
Er darf tsu lozn aun dingen a hoyz aoyf di yam
We are here for a long time
Mir zenen do far a langa tsat
I need to turn off the lights early tonight
E'ech darf faloshen di le'echt fri'et haynt ba nacht
We want to stop here
Mir vil tsu haltn do
We are from Frankfurt
Mir zenen foon Frankfurt
The same building
Di zelbr hoyz
I want to ask for permission to leave
E'ech vil tsu fregn far derloybenisht tsu lozn
I need to try this again
E'ech darf tsu prubirn duce nochamul

To open	Tsu efenen
A bit, a little, a little bit	A'bisel
To pay	Tsu batsulen
To buy	Tsu koyfen
To get to know	Tsu bakenin
Sister	Shvester
To hope	Tsu hofen
Future	Tsukunft
To live	Tsu leiben
Nice to meet you	Tzu'zeir shine tsu trefen deir
Name	Numen
Last name	Letste numen
To enter	Tsu arayn
Sad	Tzi'friden
Door	Tiya/dor

I need to open the door for my sister

E'ech darf tsu efenen di tiya far meyn shvester

I need to buy something

E'ech darf tsu koyfn epes

I want to get to know your sisters

E'ech vil tsu bakenin deyn shvester

Nice to meet you, what is your name and your last name?

Tzu'zeir shine tsu trefen deir, vos iz deiner numen aun deiner letster numen?

To hope for the better in the future

Tsu hofn far di beser in di tsukunft

Why are you sad right now?

Far vuss bist ir tzi'friden yetst?

*This *isn't* a phrase book! The purpose of this book is *solely* to provide you with the tools to create *your own* sentences!

To happen	Tsu gishayen
To order	Tsu freignen
To drink	Tsu trinken
Excuse me	Antshuldikn mir
Child	Kinder
Woman	Frow
To begin / To start	Tsu op'heyden
To finish	Tsu endikn
To help	Tsu helfn
To smoke	Tsu reychern
To love	Tsu liben
Again	Nochamul / vider

This must happen today
Duce mizz tsu gishayen haynt
Excuse me, my child is here as well
Antshuldikn mir, meyn kind iz do ochet
I love you
E'ech hob dich lib
I see you
E'ech zei dir
I need you
E'ech darf dir
I want to help
E'ech vil tsu helfen
I don't want to smoke again
E'ech vil'nisht tsu reychern nochamul
I want to learn to speak German and Yiddish
E'ech vil tsu lernen tsu reden deutsh aun yiddish

*"I love you" can also be *e'ech* hob *dir lib*.
*"*Dir*" is the direct object pronoun of the pronoun "you."

To read	Tsu leynen
To write	Tsu shrayben
To teach	Tsu lilernen
To close	Fa'machen
To choose	Tsu klayben
To prefer	Tsu beser
To put	Tsu ley'gn/ tsu shteln
Less	Aveyniker
Sun	Zin
Month	Choidesh
I Talk	E'ech red
Exact	Pinktlech
In order to	Veigen tsu

I need this book, in order to learn how to read and write in Polish.
E'ech darf duce be'yech, veigen tsu lernen vi tsu leynen aun shraybn in polish
I want to teach in Poland
E'ech vil tsu lilernen in poland
I want to close the door
E'ech vil fa'machen di tiaya
I prefer to put the gift here
E'ech beser tsu ley'gn di miton'e do
I want to pay less than you for the dinner
E'ech vil tsu tsoln veyniker vi ir far di nachtmal
I speak with the boy and the girl in Yiddish
E'ech red mit di boishik aun di meydil'e in yiddish
I see the sun today
E'ech zei di zin haynt
Is it possible to know the exact date?
Iz es meglech tsu visn di pintlech tookk?

To exchange (*money*)	Tsu vexl
To call	Tsu rufen
Brother	Brider
Dad	Tate
To sit	Tsu zitsen
Together	Tsuzamen
To change	Tsu toyshen
Of course/certainly	Doch
Welcome	Bruchim habaim
During	Bes
Years	Yu'er
Sky	Himmel
Up	Aroyf
Down	Aroop
Sorry	Antshuldigt
To follow	Tsu nechgeyn
Her	Eer
Big	Groys
New	Na'ye
Never / ever	Keynumol

I want to call my brother and my dad today
E'ech vil tsu rufen meyn brider aun meyn tate haynt
Of course I can come to the theater, and I want to sit together with you and with your sister
Doch e'ech ken kimen tsu di teater, aun e'ech vil tzitzen tsuzamen mit deer aun mit deyen shvester
I need to go down in order to see your new house
E'ech darf tsu geyn aroop in veigen tsu zen deyn na'ye hoyz
I can see the sky from the window
E'ech ken zen di himmel foon di fentster
I am sorry, however he wants to follow her to the store
E'ech bin nebechdik, ober er vil tsu nechgeyn eer tsu di shaff

To allow	Tsu lozn
To believe	Tsu gloyben
Morning	Frii/morgen
Except	Chuts
To promise	Tsu tsigizut
Good night	Git nacht
To get to know	Tsu bakenen
People	Mentshn
To move (an object)	Tsu flozen
To move (to a place)	Tsu flozen
Far	Vatt
Different	Andersh
Man	Mentsh
To return	Tsu gayne'tzrik
To receive	Tsu bakumen
Afternoon	Nochmitoog
Good afternoon	Git nochmitoog
Left / right	Linx / recht
Him / his	Aim / zeyn

I need to allow him to go with us, he is a different man now
E'ech darf tsu lozn aim tsu geyn mit aundz, er iz a andersh mentsh yetst
I believe everything except for this
E'ech gloyben alts achuts far duce
They need to get to know the people from Germany very quickly
Zey darfn tsu bakenen di mentshn foon Deutshland zeyer shnela
I need to put your cat on another chair
E'ech darf tsu shteln deyn kats aoyf andern shtul/benkel
I see the sun in the morning from the kitchen
E'ech zei di zin in di morgen fin di kech
I want this car
E'ech vil duce mashin
I must move my car to the right side of the street, because my sister needs to return home this afternoon
E'ech mizz tsu flozen meyn mashin tsu di recht zayt foon di gas, vayl meyn shvester darfn tsu gayne'tzrik tsu di hoym duce nachmitiig

*With the knowledge you've gained so far, now try to create your own sentences!

To wish	Tsu vintshen
Bad	Shlecht
To Get	Tsu bakumen
To forget	Tsu fargesen
Although	Chotsh
Everybody / Everyone	Yederin (or) alemen
To feel	Tsu filn
Past	Fargangenhayt
Next (following, after)	Vayter
To like	Tsu glachen
In front	Forent
Next (near, close)	Nuent
Behind	Hinter
Well (as in doing well)	Git
Goodbye	Zagazint
Restaurant	Restoran
Bathroom	Klozet

I don't want to wish anything bad
E'ech vilish tsu vintshn epes shlecht
I must forget everybody from my past
E'ech mizz fargesn alemen foon meyn fargangenhayt
I am close to the person behind you
E'ech bin nuent tsu di mentsh hinter di'ye
There is a person in front of me
Es iz a mentsh in forent fin mir
I say goodbye to my friends
E'ech zoog zagazint tsu meyn froynt
I want a car next year
E'ech vil a mashin vayter yu'ar

*"Bathroom" is *klozet*. (It can mean "closet" as well.)

To remove / to take out	Tsu nemen
Please	Bit'e
Beautiful	Sheyn
To lift	Tsu heyben
Include / Including	Inklude (or) chull
Belong	Geheren
To hold	Tsu halten
To check	Tsu kontrolirn
Small	Kleyn
Real	Praktish / faktish
Weather	Veter
Size	Greys
High	Hoych
Doesn't	Nisht
So (as in then)	Azoy
Correct	Re'echtik
Price	Prayz
Expensive	Tayer

She wants to remove this door, please
Zi vil tsu nemen dem tiya, bit'e
This doesn't belong here, I need to check again
Duce nish gehern do, e'ech darf tsu kontrolirn vider
This week the weather was very beautiful
Duce voch di veter iz geven zeyer sheyn
I need to know which is the real diamond
E'ech darf tsu visn vos iz di faktish diment
We need to check the size of the house
Mir darf tsu kontrolirn di greys foon di hoyz
I can pay this although the price is expensive
E'ech ken batsolnt duce chotsh di prayz iz tayer
Including everything is this price correct?
Chull alts iz dem prayz re'echtik?

BUILDING BRIDGES

In Building Bridges, we take six conjugated verbs that have been selected after studies I have conducted for several months in order to determine which verbs are most commonly conjugated, and which are then automatically followed by an infinitive verb. For example, once you know how to say, "I need," "I want," "I can," and "I like," you will be able to connect words and say almost anything you want more correctly and understandably. The following three pages contain these six conjugated verbs in first, second, third, fourth, and fifth person, as well as some sample sentences. Please master the entire program up until here prior to venturing onto this section.

I want	E'ech vil
I need	E'ech darf
I can	E'ech ken
I like	E'ech glach
I go	E'ech geyn
I have	E'ech hobn
I must / I have to	E'ech mizz

I want to go to my apartment

E'ech vil tsu geyn tsu meyn voynik

I can go with you to the bus station

E'ech ken geyn mit ir tsu di oytobus stantsye

I need to walk to the museum

E'ech darf tsu geyn tsu di muzey

I like to take the train

E'ech glach tsu nemen di ban

I am going to teach a class

E'ech ga'i tsu lernen a klas

I have to speak to my teacher

E'ech mizz tsu reden tsu meyn lerer

Please master pages #17-#39, prior to attempting the following pages!

You want / do you want? - Di vist / di vist?
He wants / does he want - Er vil / er vil?
She wants / does she want - Zi vil / zi vil?
We want / do we want - Mir vist / mir vist?
They want / do they want - Zey vil / zey vil?
You (plural) want - Alle vist / alle vist?

You need / do you need - Ir darf / ir darf?
He needs / does he need - Er darf / er darf?
She needs / does she need - Zi darf / zi darf?
We want / do we want - Mir vil / mir vil?
They need / do they need - Zey darf / zey darf?
You (plural) need - Alle darfst / alle darfst?

You can / can you - Ir ken / ir ken?
He can / can he - Er ken / er ken?
She can / can she - Zi ken / zi ken?
We can / can we - Mir kenin / mir kenin?
They can / can they - Zey ken / zey ken?
You (plural) can - Alle kenst / alle kenst?

You like / do you like - Ir glach / ir glacht
He likes / does he like - Er glacht / er glacht?
She like / does she like - Zi glacht / zi glacht?
We like / do we like - Mir glacht / mir glacht?
They like / do they like - Zey glacht / zey glacht?
You (plural) like - Alle glachen / alle glachen?

You go / do you go - Ir geyt / ir geyn?
He goes / does he go - Er geyt / er geyn?
She goes / does she go - Zi geyt / zi geyn?
We go / do we go - Mir geyt / mir geyn?
They go / do they go - Zey geyten / zey geyn?
You (plural) go - Alle geytst / alle geytst?

You have / do you have - Ir hostz / ir hostz?
He has / does he have - Er hoss / er hoss?
She has / does she have - Zi hoss / zi hoss?
We have / do we have - Mir hoss / mir hoss?
They have / do they have - Zey hoss / zey hoss?
You (plural) have - Alle hoben / Alle hoben?

Please master pages #17-#39, prior to attempting the following!

Do you want to go?
Di vist geyn?
He wants to fly
Er vist tsu flyen
We want to swim
Mir vist tsu shvimen
Do they want to run?
Du zalst zey vist tsu loyfen?
Do you need to clean?
Di darfst tsu kleynen?
She needs to sing a song
Zi darf tsu zingen a lid
We need to travel
Mir darf tsu arumforn
They don't need to fight
Zey darfish tsu kreygn'zein
You (plural) need to see this film
Alle Darf tsu zen duce film
Can you hear me?
Di kenst mech hern?
He can dance very well
Er ken tantsn zeyer git
We can go out tonight
Mir kenin geyn aoys haynt ba nacht
They can break the wood
Zey ken brechn di holts
Do you like to eat here?
Ir glach tsu esn do?

He likes to spend time here
Er glach tsu farbrengen tsat do
We like to fix the house
Mir glachen di shtyb zu reparyeren
They like to cook
Zey glachen tsu kochen
You (plural) like my house
Alle glachts mein hoytz
Do you go to school today?
Di geyst tsu shule haynt?
He goes fishing
Er geyt fishin
We are going to see the moon
Mir zenen gegangen zen di levuna
Do you have money?
Tsi ir hobn gelt?
He needs to go to sleep
Er darf tsu geyn tsu shlofn
She must look outside
Zi mizz kiken aroys
We must sign our names
Mir mizz shraben our numen
They must send the letter
Zey mizz shikn di briv
You (plural) must order
Alle mizz freignen
(*freignen* can also means *ask*)

Other Useful Tools in the Yiddish Language

Months - Chudshim

January	Yanuar
February	Februar
March	Marts
April	April
May	May
June	Iuni
July	Iuli
August	Oygust
September	September
October	Oktober
November	November
December	Detsember

Days of the Week - Teg foon di voch

Sunday	Zuntik
Monday	Mantik
Tuesday	Dinstag
Wednesday	Mitvach
Thursday	Donershtag
Friday	Freytik
Saturday	Shabes

Directions - Instruktsyes

North	Tsofn
South	Drum
East	Mizrach
West	Merb

Seasons - Tseytn

Spring	Friling'
Summer	Zumer
Autumn	Harbst
Winter	Vinter

Colors - Kolors

Black	Shvartse
White	Veyse
Gray	Groy
Red	Royt
Blue	Bloy
Yellow	Gale
Green	Grin
Orange	Marants
Purple	Lila
Pink	Rozeve
Brown	Broyn

Numbers - Numern

One	Eynst	Twenty	Tsvantsik
Two	Tsvey	Thirty	Draysik
Three	Drey	Forty	Fertsik
Four	Fir	Fifty	Fuftsik
Five	Finf	Sixty	Zekhtsik
Six	Zex	Seventy	Zibetsik
Seven	Zibn	Eighty	Akhtsik
Eight	Acht	Ninety	Nayntsik
Nine	Neyn	Hundred	Hundert
Ten	Tsen	Thousand	Toyznt
		Million	Milyan

CONCLUSION

Congratulations! You have completed all the tools needed to master the Yiddish language, and I hope that this has been a valuable learning experience. Now you have sufficient communication skills to be confident enough to embark on a visit to Israel or Brooklyn, impress your friends, and boost your resume so good luck.

This program is available in other languages as well, and it is my fervent hope that my language learning programs will be used for good, enabling people from all corners of the globe and from all cultures and religions to be able to communicate harmoniously. After memorizing the required three hundred and fifty words, please perform a daily five-minute exercise by creating sentences in your head using these words. This simple exercise will help you grasp conversational communications even more effectively. Also, once you memorize the vocabulary on each page, follow it by using a notecard to cover the words you have just memorized and test yourself and follow that by going back and using this same notecard technique on the pages you studied during the previous days. This repetition technique will assist you in mastering these words in order to provide you with the tools to create your own sentences.

Every day, use this notecard technique on the words that you have just studied.

Everything in life has a catch. The catch here is just consistency. If you just open the book, and after the first few pages of studying the program, you put it down, then you will not gain anything. However, if you consistently dedicate a half hour daily to studying, as well as reviewing what you have learned from previous days, then you will quickly realize why this method is the most effective technique ever created to become conversational in a foreign language. My technique works! For anyone who doubts this technique, all I can say is that it has worked for me and hundreds of others.

NOTE FROM THE AUTHOR

Thank you for your interest in my work. I encourage you to share your overall experience of this book by posting a review. Your review can make a difference! Please feel free to describe how you benefited from my method or provide creative feedback on how I can improve this program. I am constantly seeking ways to enhance the quality of this product, based on personal testimonials and suggestions from individuals like you.
Thanks and best of luck,
Yatir Nitzany

Printed in Great Britain
by Amazon